WHISTLE ONE

Whistle One
Poems

Shania Kohn Brown

The Hermit Kingdom Press
Cheltenham ✶ Seoul ✶ Bangalore ✶ Cebu

The Hermit Kingdom Press
3741 Walnut Street, Suite 407
Philadelphia, Pennsylvania 19104
United States of America
http://www.TheHermitKingdomPress.com

© 2004 by Shania Kohn Brown

All rights reserved. No part of this book may be reproduced in any form or by any means, electronic or mechanical, including photocopying, recording, or by any information storage and retrieval system, without permission in writing from the publisher.

ISBN 1-59689-000-2

WHISTLE ONE: POEMS

FOR ALL WHO SEEK JUSTICE

Contents

Setting

"I Heard It" -- 17

"Back" -- 20

"You See What I See" -- 21

"Human Camera" -- 23

"Eyes On My Back" -- 24

"Pride" -- 26

"Turning The Other Cheek" -- 27

"It Does Not Matter" -- 29

"Animal In A Cage" -- 30

"Whistle Traumatized" -- 33

"Monkey" -- 35

Escalation

"Intensify" -- 41

"Guilt Propels" -- 42

"To Forget" -- 44

"Justify" -- 47

"Why?" -- 50

"The Test" -- 52

"The Loss" -- 54

"The Loss 2" -- 56

"Time" -- 58

"Space" -- 60

"Gravity" -- 63

"Cries" -- 64

"Spurs" -- 68

"Empty Road" -- 69

"Up On High" -- 71

"Slave Owners' Club" -- 73

Whistle One

Poems

"He lifts up a banner for the distant nations, he whistles for those at the ends of the earth. Here they come swiftly and speedily!"

Isaiah 5:26

Setting

"I Heard It"

I heard it
As my eyes opened
And wandered
Through space

                    And time
                    In a daze --
                    A short moment
                    After the awaking.

The morning calm
Was invaded
Like a battle opening
On that frightful morning

                    In Pearl Harbor.
                    The morning calm
                    Broken,
                    Shattered

By invading planes,
Firing,
Shooting,
And dropping bombs

                    From the sky.
                    Peace was
                    Shattered
                    And calm was

No more.
It was my
Pearl Harbor –
That day.

        A shrill
        Whistle
        Broke
        The morning

Calm.
Out of nowhere
A battle cry
Was raised.

        It was a surprise
        Attack.
        I opened my eyes
        Wider

In order to see
From where
The attacks came
So mercilessly.

        But I could not see.
        I only heard
        As I lay awake
        Rudely shocked.

And the bombs came
Down
With a battle cry –
The aggressive whistle.

"Back"

My eyes rolled back
Behind my head?

So what?
What's it to you?

So
You think you can take out your whip?

You think you have the right to whip me
With your whistle?

Who made me your slave?
Who made you my slave master?

"You See What I See"

You see what I see.
I see.

Does that make you feel like a god –
That you see all that I see?

Will you be the god of me?
Will you enforce your rules on me?

These are your rules.
They do not make sense to me.

You see what I see.
I see.

Do you have to remind me
That you see what I see?

You feel the need to show
That you are the god of me?

You want me to know
That you know all that I do?

You see what I see.
I see.

Does that make you a god?
Or are you just a voyeur?

"Human Camera"

You look at me.
But you do not see me.

You see a transparency.
You see a transparent camera.

It is a human camera that you see –
A camera in a human body.

And you want a photo
Of you.

You want your face
On the screen.

You do not care
If you hurt me.

"Eyes On My Back"

Do I have eyes on my back?
Can I see before me

And behind me?
I don't have eyes

On my sides either.
I am a human being

With eyes to see what is before me.
If I look this way,

Then my back will be turned
In the opposite direction.

I can only see what is in front of me.
I do not have eyes on my back.

When I face someone,
My back will be to someone else.

I am a human being
Who is biologically built as a human being.

"Pride"

Why does he not look at me?
Why is his back turned?

I am proud of myself,
You know.

My pride will not permit
His back turned

Towards me.
My pride demands

He face me
Right now,

                                          At this very minute,
                                             This very second.

                                                    Look at me!
                                        Hear my whistle roar

                                                  Like a lion
                                        Defending her pride.

"Turning The Other Cheek"

I will not turn
My other cheek.
Certainly not!

When your back is turned,
I will whistle
And annoy you 'till no end.

There will be
No turning
The other cheek.

You have wronged me
With your
Back,

And I will torture
You
With my whistle.

Don't expect me
To turn my
Other cheek.

I will slap you hard
On your other cheek
With my whistle.

"It Does Not Matter"

It does not matter
That I am not really there.

    I see through my screen.
    I hear through my ear piece.

        I know that you are not
        Looking at me.

            I know that your back
            Is turned.

                And through the TV screen
                I will harass you.

                    I will whistle
                    Until you are thoroughly peeved.

"Animal In A Cage"

You are to me
Like an animal in a cage.
You are there
For my amusement.

I don't care that
You are human
And not an animal.
You amuse me.

I am bored.
My life is boring.
You entertain me
In your little cage.

I will tap on the bars
To get your attention.
You are to me
Like an animal in a cage.

I will whistle in your direction
To get you to look at me.
I am bored.
And you amuse me.

I see you walking.
I see you sitting.
I see you typing away.
I see you eating.

You are like an animal
In a cage
For all to see.
I am entertained.

I see you when you awake.
I watch you falling asleep.
I hear you cry.
And I am amused.

I see you
Like an animal in a cage.
Although you are human
I will treat you like you are not.

To me
You are amusement.
You entertain me.
I am not bored because of you.

Who cares
That you are in a cage?
You entertain.
You amuse.

Who cares that
You suffer?
I am not bored.
I enjoy watching.

You are like
An animal in a cage.
Your little cage
Provides fun amusement.

"Whistle Traumatized"

You know that
The whistle traumatized.
You know what happened
At the old place.

Like brown
Trees
Devoid of leaves
In winter time,

I have suffered
In the brownness
Of the heartless
Whistle.

The whistle –
It became a
Symbol,
A metaphor.

Like a whip
The whistle
Was used.
The whistle

Is the name of the horrible
Whip –
Painful
And meant to torture.

Yea,
The whistle
Is
More –

More
Than
A symbol
And a metaphor.

The whistle
Inflicted pain –
Real pain
That caused tears to flow.

Every whistle
Whips
Like the first whistle
That was used to inflict pain.

The whistle
Traumatized.
Your whistle
Traumatizes.

And you sit there
Lofty and self-righteous,
Like you have done
Nothing wrong.

Like the slave drivers
Who used to whip
Humans
Thinking that it was their right.

"Monkey"

Like a monkey
I will copy.
I will imitate
Your whistle.

You whistle,
So I whistle.
If you whistle,
It must be okay.

You whistle.
I whistle.
We all whistle.
We all wash our hands in it.

We whistle together
Like monkeys
In a tree party
Inside the Amazon jungle.

And that makes it all right.
No matter
That we are targeting
Our whistle.

It isn't wrong
That we
Pick him out
For the whistle treatment.

I will monkey-copy.
You whistled,
And I will join your
Monkey Whistling Club.

I will follow you
And whistle.
When do you whistle?
I will whistle likewise.

Am I not expected to whistle?
Not whistling,
Won't I be outside the club?
I will monkey-copy.

No matter how
He feels.
I will follow you
And whistle.

I will be a monkey
To join
The Monkey Whistling Club.
I don't want to be left out.

You whistle.
I whistle.
We all whistle.
And that makes it okay.

Like a monkey
I will copy.
I will imitate
Your whistle.

Escalation

"Intensify"

The solution
Must surely be
To intensify.
Keep whistling.

More he hears
The whistle,
The more
He'll get used to it.

Isn't it like
When a husband
Beats on his wife?
The more he

Beats her,
The more she gets
Used to it.
So keep whistling.

The more you whip
Someone,
Doesn't he develop
Toughness in his skin?

So intensify!
Keep whistling!
He'll get used to it.
The solution is to intensify.

"Guilt Propels"

I feel guilty.
I whistled
And I caused him pain.
I know and I feel guilty.

What course of action should I follow?
Should I stop whistling?
Should I stop causing him pain?
How can I assuage my guilty feeling?

What if others whistled?
Would I not feel better?
I won't be the only one.
I will be one of many.

I know that I will not feel so guilty.
How will I get others to whistle?
What should I say?
What conditions should I create?

I know I won't feel so guilty
If others join in.
We'll be a part of the group.
The guilt will be divided.

I won't be the only one guilty.
I won't be merely one of the few.
How can I get people to whistle
So that I will be one of many?

"To Forget"

How can I forget?
How can I remember no more?
How can I move on
If you keep reminding me

Of the pain,
The past experience of
Suffering
And injustice?

Don't you know
That every time
You whistle,
I remember?

I remember
The pain I experienced,
The injustice
That covered me,

And the silence
Of those who watched
Quietly with a lack of courage
As wrong was done.

Every whistle reminds,
Makes me remember
The proto-whistle
Used as a whip.

Your whistle
Marks again
Over the scars
Inflicted over there.

It is the pain of the past
That your whistle
Re-opens
And reminds.

How can I forget?
When you all
Keep whistling?
How can I move on?

The drunken man
Beats his wife
Again and again
Without mercy.

Does his lack of cognition
Excuse his inflicting of pain?
You know the pain of the past.
Why do you persist in adding to it?

Why do you whip
Like they did
Way back when.
I should certainly have forgotten.

But I can't
Because you force me
To remember
The pain.

Daily
You remind me of the pain
That is past
But lives again and again

In
Your whistle
Jointed by others
Who imitate.

To forget
Becomes impossible
With daily reminders
Forcing me to remember.

Why won't you help me
To forget the pain,
To look forward
To the future?

Why do you whip
With your whistle
And force me to remember,
To experience pain perpetually?

To forget,
That's what I want to do
For my sake –
But more so for theirs.

But you won't let me forget.
Their guilt continues
In the daily reminder
And the debt grows.

"Justify"

What would you like to do?
Would you like to justify
Their guilt?
Is that why you whistle?

If you whistle,
Does that make
Past wrongs
Okay?

Don't you see?
Your whistle
Does not justify
Them.

Your whistle
Convicts them.
It reminds their wrong
And the precedent set.

Their wrong is intensified
In your whistle
Like a domino effect.
More guilt is added.

Like a small snowball
That becomes bigger and bigger
With more snow added,
Their guilt increases.

Yes, indeed.
Whistle multiplies
Like the multiplication
Of wrongs.

Their wrongs,
Forgiven once,
Forgiven twice,
Seventy times seven,

Keep growing.
Daily
Their wrongs gain
Greater significance
In your reminder.

You whistle
And remind.
They are guilty!
They are guilty!

What they did
Is unforgivable!
Look at the consequences –
The domino effect!

No, you do not justify.
They do not find
Forgetfulness;
Only reminders of their guilt.

"Why?"

Why do you persist?
Do you whistle to help
Or to harm?
Does it matter?

What effect does it have
On me?
Don't you know?
It causes extreme pain.

Memories of pain
Rise up
Like a phoenix
Bent on righteous vengeance.

Like a husband
Deprived of his loving wife,
The soul-mate meant for life
Taken away from him,

I feel the pain
As I hear your whistle.
I remember what happened.
The loss I suffered.

Why?
Why do you persist?
Why are you bent on causing pain?
Why continue to add to suffering?

Is it vanity?
Is it because you want to hurt me?
Do you want to "liberate" me?
Do you want to imprison me?

Why?
Why do you persist?
Don't you know
What you are doing?

You remind me of my loss.
You make me remember
What I had to give up.
You make me feel pain

All over again.
Why?
Why do you persist?
Don't you know?

It doesn't matter
What your intentions
Are –
Noble or not.

Your whistle
Has the same effect on me
To make me remember
My loss.

"The Test"

It's a sick test –
The Whistle Test.
Who created it
Anyway?

What is the test supposed to accomplish?
If a wife-beating husband
Beats his wife
Then she should act favorably towards him?

Is the Whistle Test
Like the Wife Beating Test
To see that she truly loves him?
Inflict pain to see?

Is the Whistle Test
A protective measure?
If there's a lot of whistling,
He will be discouraged.

He will be reluctant to commit,
And that suits
Because I am afraid to commit.
Is that what the Whistle Test is for?

The Test
Where the goal of happiness is discouraged,
Repulsive measures are fully raised –
What's its positive purpose?

"The Loss"

What was lost
Because of the whistle?

Years back
In the land of Providence

Were emptied
Silos filled with grain

In a conflict
Intensified by the whistle.

Whistle sounded the
Trumpet,

Signaling the start of a war
As in the olden days.

Injustice inflicted
Was never rectified,

Upsetting the cosmic order
With Justice demanding

Restoration.
The harvest was taken

With no regard for God
Or fear of Him.

Labor done for God
To honor him

Was made into nothing
Like the dew on the morning

Grass
Evaporating

At the light of day
As the sun shines brightly above.

Hours and hours of work
Planting and tending

Great effort exerted
To gather the harvest

Were made into naught
Like a baby left unattended

For hours and hours
Even as the infant

Cried for mommy
Who was nowhere to be seen.

The Worker who labored,
Exerted with all that he had

Was left in the dust
As the storeroom of the

Harvest
Was taken over.

Whistles marked
The unjust loss.

"The Loss 2"

The whistle
Reminds

Of the years past
Hard-exerted labor

And the loss
Of years of labor.

Like digging a well
And then being forced to move

To dig another well,
The well was stolen

And again
A new well dug

To be taken
With no regard to the

Laborer.
It was there

All the while –
The whistle.

A whistle
To mark the injustice

To sound the
Loss

"Time"

Time passes,
Yet remains

                                        Still
                              In the whistle.

Like a timeless
Foundation myth

                         That is recited over
                            And over again

The whistle resounds
Over and over again

                     As in a prophetic doom
                     Sung over and over again

By seers
Who are appointed by God.

                            Like a cosmic plan
                    Designed before the foundation

Of the earth,
The pattern is repeated

                    In the blowing of the whistle
                    As the world goes towards

A Prophetic
End.

                                        Time stands still
                                        As events occur

In the mythic symbol --
A prophetic metaphor.

                                        Time is conjoined
                                 Like a twin united in one

To the epic story
And a mythic end

                                  As unconscious prophets
                           Whistle the untranslatable oracle.

Time is lost,
Time is gained,

                                            Time remains –
                        All within the prophetic time-line.

"Space"

The whistle resounds
In profane space

In the original wrong
Committed in a godless place.

Yet,
The whistle

Is not confined
In the profane space;

The whistle infiltrates
The sacred space

Like a soldier
Entering the church

To kill his enemy
Who seeks refuge

In the House of God.
There is no regard for God.

There is no respect for
The Holy Place.

The whistle invades
The holy ground,

A worshipping place
Of the Living God.

The profane wrong
Enters the sacred realm,

And the sacred space
Is defiled.

There is none penitent.
No prayers are offered to ask

God
For His pardon

For the wrongs committed
In His House.

Space
No longer exists in duality;

The sacred has been broken
By the profane.

The whistle
Sounds

Throughout the sacred space,
Resounding the wrong

Originally committed in the profane realm.
And none repent.

No one is sorry
Or wants to make real amends.

The wrong remains
In the transcendent space.

"Gravity"

Gravity
Pulls

Like a magnet
Beckoning a metal.

All that is thrown up in the air
Crashes down against the floor

With a thump
Like a meteor falling from the sky

Creating a big hole on earth,
A sight to behold.

Such is a whistle –
A gravity that inevitably pulls,

A meteor that inevitably creates a big hole,
And a missile fired that will certainly explode.

The whistle pulls us
More and more

Towards that epic conclusion –
The corruption of decency,

Freedom,
And all that is good.

"Cries"

A mother cries
Uncontrollable tears
As her baby dies
In her arms.

A babe,
So innocent,
Filled with smiles
Just days before,

Remains weak
With life leaving him –
No smiles to be found
On his cherub face.

The mother loves
Her little baby boy
Who is helpless
And weak.

Images of his smiles,
His cries,
And his walking
Flash before her eyes.

And tears flow
Down her maternal face
Filled with concern
And sorrow

For the coming death
Of her newborn babe
Who brought her
So much joy.

The babe,
So fragile
And so dependent,
Is too feeble to cry.

So the mother cries
For the both of them,
Tears rolling down
Her beautiful face

As her body heaves
In the pain of her heart –
Her arms hold fast
To stabilize the babe

In his last moment of
Life.
There he is –
So helpless.

And the whistle is heard
Outside.
Shrill and heartless,
Jeering whistle

Breaks the calm of the morning sun
In the last moments of the helpless babe.
The gentle mother
Feels her tears boil

Like an egg broken
On a burning-hot frying pan.
She detects,
So she thinks,

A wincing of pain
In the dying babe's face –
A helpless look
Marked by intruding pain.

And the mother feels
Her heart beat
In anger
And her cries become louder

As the thoughtless
Whistle
Resounds
Outside

With no concern
For the dying babe
In the last moments
Of his life

Or for the mom
Who
Cries
Tears that only a mother can.

"Spurs"

The rider of the horse
Digs her spurs deeper
And deeper in.
The blood flows

From the poor horse
That exists for her.
Mercilessly she plunges
The spurs

Like a dagger
Thrust into a lover
In a fit of jealous rage.
The horse winces in pain.

Go faster!
Go faster!
The sharp spurs
Seem to cry.

Like a shrill whistle
That breaks
The beautiful quiet
Of a moon-lit summer night,

The spurs
Interrupt
The peaceful enjoyment
Of the gentle horse.

"Empty Road"

The road is
Empty,
So it seems;

For,
There is nothing
In sight —

No human beings,
No cars,
No animals.

There's only the road —
And the walls
That parallel the road.

I walk
With my guards fully down
Thinking about the beauty of the world,

Lost in a daydream,
With hopes for the future,
Not giving a thought to the empty road.

Suddenly,
My idyllic world is interrupted,
Like the bombing in Pearl Harbor.

A shrill whistle
Intrudes
Out of nowhere.

"Up On High"

Who are they
Who work on high?
Can they see me
From up there?

Surely,
They will have difficulty
Making out my face –
Certainly,

They cannot see
The way my eye balls move.
They can't see
From up on high.

Yet,
They seem to see,
And they whistle
On cue.

Do they know me?
I surely do not know them?
Do they own me?
They seem to think so.

I owe them
Nothing.
I don't even
Know them.

And they have no right
Over me
As if they were divine beings.
They waxed proud.

They are working.
They should carry on working.
What business is it
Of theirs

That I walk
Below
Here
As a pedestrian

Minding
My own business
Thinking about work
And looking ahead?

They should work.
I should walk.
They owe me nothing.
And I owe them nothing.

They need not look at me.
I need not look at them.
There is no obligation.
We are all free.

"Slave Owners' Club"

They think they belong to
Slave Owners' Club.
They take out their whip
And whistle away.

Is it right
Just because they all do it?
Is it righteous
Because they all participate in the whipping?

The slave
Remains
With whiplashes
Imprinted

On his body
And heart.
Pain permeates
His being.

Slave Owners' Club
Members
Hold onto their whip
And console themselves over pleasant conversation

And nice biscuits
Accompanying choice tea.
They give no thought
To the pain that they have inflicted.

About the Author:

Shania Kohn Brown is an American who often travels in Europe. Her literary work reflects her concerns for social justice and human rights. This is her first book of poems.

www.ingramcontent.com/pod-product-compliance
Lightning Source LLC
Chambersburg PA
CBHW051713040426
42446CB00008B/861